JESUS LOVES YOU

Contact Us:

✉ MyBibleWorkbooks@gmail.com

📷 Projectkingdomcome

f Projectkingdomcome

PROJECT KINGDOM COME
ISBN 978-1-961786-07-3

Get The Entire Workbook Series!

THE BOOK OF **GENESIS**
BIBLE-BASED WORKBOOK
PROJECT KINGDOM COME

THE BOOKS OF **EXODUS & JOSHUA**
BIBLE-BASED WORKBOOK
PROJECT KINGDOM COME

THE BOOKS OF **I & II SAMUEL**
BIBLE-BASED WORKBOOK
PROJECT KINGDOM COME

THE BOOKS OF **I & II KINGS**
BIBLE-BASED WORKBOOK
PROJECT KINGDOM COME

THE BOOKS OF **ESTHER & RUTH**
BIBLE-BASED WORKBOOK
PROJECT KINGDOM COME

THE BOOKS OF **DANIEL & JOB**
BIBLE-BASED WORKBOOK
PROJECT KINGDOM COME

THE BOOK OF **MATTHEW**
BIBLE-BASED WORKBOOK
PROJECT KINGDOM COME

THE BOOK OF **MARK**
BIBLE-BASED WORKBOOK
PROJECT KINGDOM COME

THE BOOK OF **LUKE**
BIBLE-BASED WORKBOOK
PROJECT KINGDOM COME

THE BOOK OF **JOHN**
BIBLE-BASED WORKBOOK
PROJECT KINGDOM COME

THE BOOK OF **ACTS**
BIBLE-BASED WORKBOOK
PROJECT KINGDOM COME

THE BOOK OF **REVELATION**
BIBLE-BASED WORKBOOK
PROJECT KINGDOM COME

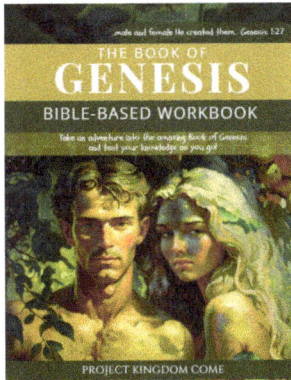

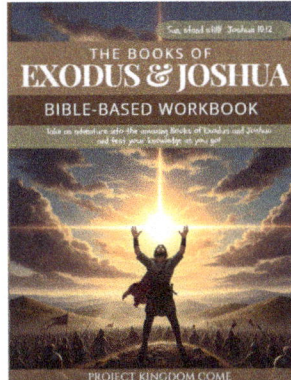

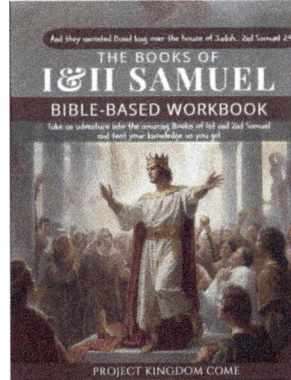

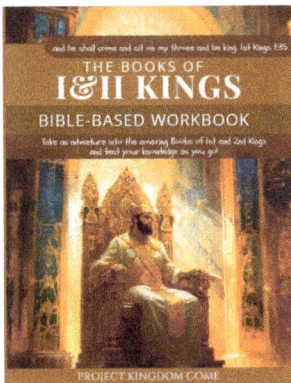

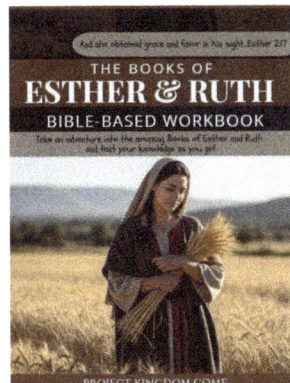

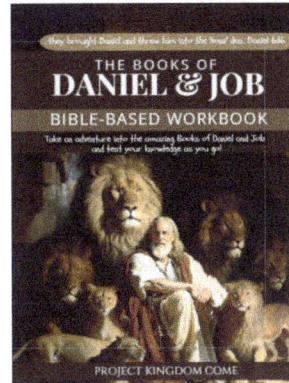

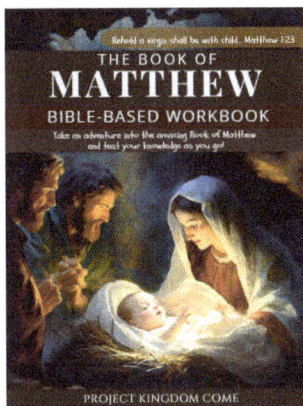

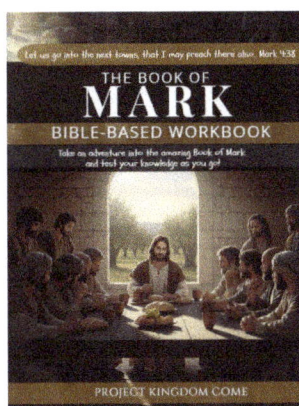

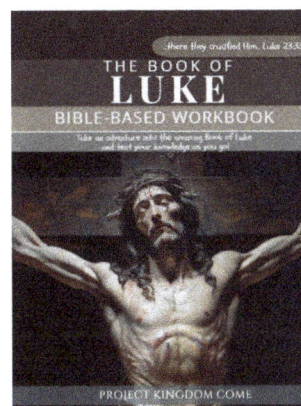

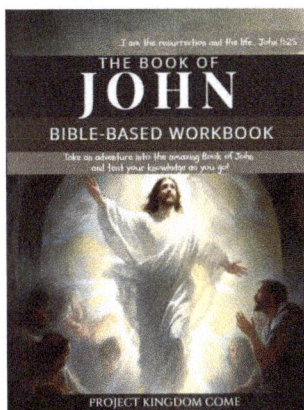

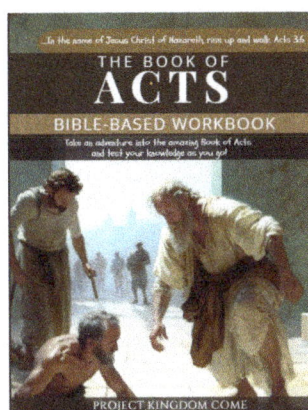

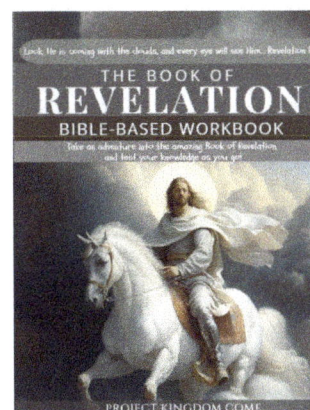

WWW.MYBIBLEWORKBOOKS.COM

PROJECT KINGDOM COME

This workbook belongs to:

_____

_____

_____

Leave your mark!

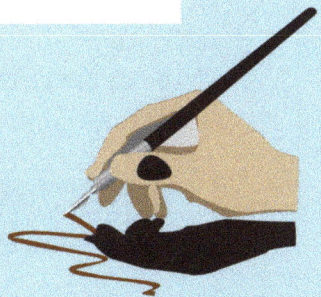

HOW TO USE THIS WORKBOOK

This workbook is designed to help young people explore the treasures in God's Word while having fun, growing in faith, and learning how to search the Scriptures for life's answers.

Here is what you will find inside:

Multiple Choice Questions
Each question comes directly from Scripture and includes a reference verse to help with locating the answer in the Bible. If possible, use a physical Bible to search for the answers.

Weekly Segments
Questions are grouped in weekly categories that could also be completed in a shorter or longer time frame.

Weekly Memory Verses
At the start of every week is a Bible verse to memorize. Each day of that week will repeat that memory verse with a chance to test memorization at the end of the week.

Certificate of Completion
At the end of the workbook, please find a Certificate of Achievement, ready for the child's name and parent or teacher's signature. Celebrate the accomplishment of studying an entire book in the Bible!

Answer Key
The workbook contains an answer key to serve as a support tool for parents or teachers reviewing the responses.

Recommendation for Parents and/or Teachers: Review the responses with your child or student and discuss lessons learned or interesting insights, to improve the child's retention and enrichment in the knowledge of God's word.

You can do all things through Christ who gives you strength!
Philippians 4:13

SAMPLE QUESTION...
HOW TO USE THIS WORKBOOK

Reading the reference verse will always lead you to the correct answer!

In the beginning was: (John 1:1)

A The Word
B. Heaven and Earth
C. Heaven only
D. Earth only

The number that comes after the book is the 'Chapter'

This is the name of a book in the Bible

John 1:1

The number after the chapter is the 'Verse'

NOW TEST YOURSELF! FIND JOSHUA CHAPTER 1 VERSE 8 IN YOUR BIBLE!

INTRODUCTION: THE BOOK OF MARK

Jesus the Servant King - Full of Power, Compassion, and Action

The **Book of Mark** is the shortest of the four Gospels — but don't let that fool you. It moves fast and takes you straight into the action of Jesus' life and ministry. Written by **John Mark (a close friend of Peter),** this Gospel is like a highlight reel of the **miracles, teachings, and bold compassion of Jesus.**

Mark shows us that Jesus didn't just talk about the Kingdom of God — He lived it. He **healed the sick**, **calmed storms, raised the dead**, and **set people free**. And through it all, **He served others with love and humility**.

As you go through this workbook, you will discover:
- **Jesus has power over sickness, nature, and even death**
- **Jesus cares deeply for the hurting and the forgotten**
- **Jesus came not to be served, but to serve**
- **Faith isn't just something you believe — it's something you live**
- **Following Jesus means boldly sharing His love with the world**

Mark's Gospel is fast-paced, full of awe, and centered on who Jesus is and what He came to do — **to rescue, restore, and reign.**

Get ready to meet the Servant King and watch your faith come alive — one miracle at a time!

"For even the Son of Man did not come to be served, but to serve, and to give His life as a ransom for many." - Mark 10:45

WEEK 1

1. Who was in the wilderness preaching a baptism of repentance for the forgiveness of sins? (Mark 1:4)

A. Jesus
B. The Holy Spirit
C. Peter
D. John the Baptist

2. Where did John the Baptist conduct his baptisms? (Mark 1:5)

A. River Nile
B. River Jordan
C. In Galilee
D. The Red Sea

3. Who was John the Baptist referring to when he said he was not worthy to untie the strap of His sandals? (Mark 1:1–7)

A. Jesus
B. The Holy Spirit
C. Mark
D. Matthew

WEEK 1 MEMORY VERSE: MARK 8:34
When He had called the people to Himself, with His disciples also, He said to them, "Whoever desires to come after Me, let him deny himself, and take up his cross, and follow Me.

WEEK 1

4. John said he baptized with water, but the One coming after him would baptize with what? (Mark 1:7–8)

A. Oil
B. The Holy Spirit
C. Prayers
D. Blessings

5. What happened when Jesus was baptized by John in the Jordan? (Mark 1:9–11)

A. The heavens opened
B. The Spirit descended on Him like a dove
C. A voice from heaven declared, "You are My beloved Son, in whom I am well pleased."
D. All the above

6. How long was Jesus in the wilderness, being tempted by Satan? (Mark 1:13)

A. For a little while
B. Forty days
C. A week
D. Four weeks

WEEK 1 MEMORY VERSE: MARK 8:34

When He had called the people to Himself, with His disciples also, He said to them, "Whoever desires to come after Me, let him deny himself, and take up his cross, and follow Me.

WEEK 1

7. In which region did Jesus begin preaching the gospel of the Kingdom of God? (Mark 1:14–15)

A. Galilee

B. Jerusalem

C. Judea

D. Bethlehem

8. What did Jesus say to Simon and Andrew as He saw them casting a net into the Sea of Galilee? (Mark 1:16–17)

A. Follow Me, and I will show you a better trade

B. Leave your father and mother and follow Me

C. Whoever does not give up everything cannot be My disciple

D. Follow Me, and I will make you become fishers of men

9. Which brothers did Jesus call after Simon and Andrew? (Mark 1:19)

A. James and John

B. Mark and James

C. Peter and John

D. Peter and James

WEEK 1 MEMORY VERSE: MARK 8:34

When He had called the people to Himself, with His disciples also, He said to them, "Whoever desires to come after Me, let him deny himself, and take up his cross, and follow Me.

WEEK 1

10. **Why were people astonished at Jesus' teaching? (Mark 1:22)**

A. Because He taught in parables
B. Because He taught with great wisdom
C. Because He taught with authority, not like the scribes
D. Because He taught them things they had never heard

11. **Why didn't Jesus allow the demons to speak as He cast them out? (Mark 1:34)**

A. They were rude
B. They were tormenting people
C. They knew who He was
D. They had nothing good to say

12. **Why could Jesus no longer enter the towns openly to preach? (Mark 1:40–45)**

A. Because the man He healed of leprosy told everyone, and huge crowds came to see Jesus from everywhere
B. Because people were trying to harm Him
C. Because Jesus wanted more quiet time
D. Because He didn't want too much attention

WEEK 1 MEMORY VERSE: MARK 8:34

When He had called the people to Himself, with His disciples also, He said to them, "Whoever desires to come after Me, let him deny himself, and take up his cross, and follow Me.

WEEK 1

13. What did the friends of the paralytic man do to get him to Jesus? (Mark 2:2–4)

A. Pushed through the crowd
B. Shouted for mercy
C. The disciples helped them
D. Uncovered the roof and lowered the man down

14. Why did the scribes accuse Jesus of blasphemy? (Mark 2:6–7)

A. Because He said He could forgive sins
B. Because He healed on the Sabbath
C. Because He had power
D. All the above

15. How did Jesus respond when criticized for eating with sinners and tax collectors? (Mark 2:15–17)

A. The sick need a doctor, not those who are well
B. I came to call sinners, not the righteous
C. Both A and B
D. None of the above

WEEK 1 MEMORY VERSE: MARK 8:34
When He had called the people to Himself, with His disciples also, He said to them, "Whoever desires to come after Me, let him deny himself, and take up his cross, and follow Me.

WEEK 1

16. What was Jesus' response when asked why His disciples did not fast? (Mark 2:18–20)

A. Can friends of the bridegroom fast while He is with them?
B. The time will come when the bridegroom is taken away, then they will fast
C. Jesus did not answer
D. Both A and B

17. What happens if someone sews unshrunk cloth on an old garment? (Mark 2:21)

A. The patch strengthens the old garment
B. It shows we can mix the old and the new
C. The new patch pulls away from the old cloth, and the tear becomes worse
D. It creates a new garment from the old one

18. What happens if new wine is put into old wineskins? (Mark 2:22)

A. The wine spoils because the skins are too old
B. The old wineskins expand to fit the new wine
C. The wineskins burst, and both the wine and the skins are ruined
D. The new wine loses its strength and becomes like the old

WEEK 1 MEMORY VERSE: MARK 8:34

When He had called the people to Himself, with His disciples also, He said to them, "Whoever desires to come after Me, let him deny himself, and take up his cross, and follow Me.

WEEK 1

19. How did Jesus respond to the Pharisees when they questioned the disciples for picking grain on the Sabbath? (Mark 2:23–28)

A. David ate the consecrated bread
B. The Sabbath was made for man
C. The Son of Man is Lord of the Sabbath
D. All the above

20. Why were the Scribes and Pharisees watching Jesus closely in the synagogue? (Mark 3:1–6)

A. To see if He would heal the man with the withered hand
B. So they could accuse Him if He healed on the Sabbath
C. Both A and B
D. Because they were jealous of Him

21. How many disciples (apostles) did Jesus appoint? (Mark 3:14)

A. Seven
B. Ten
C. Three
D. Twelve

WEEK 1 MEMORY VERSE: MARK 8:34
When He had called the people to Himself, with His disciples also, He said to them, "Whoever desires to come after Me, let him deny himself, and take up his cross, and follow Me.

"

My God strengthens me and helps me (Isaiah 41:10)

"

Great job completing the week!

**Did you memorize the daily verse?
Test yourself by writing it here...**

_____

_____

_____

_____

_____

_____

**Use this space to draw a scene from the Bible or reflect
on something you learned, felt or experienced...**

22. Why did Jesus appoint apostles? (Mark 3:14-15)

A. That they might be with Him
B. That He might send them out to preach,
C. That He may give them the power to heal sicknesses and to cast out demons
D. All the above

23. What new name did Jesus give to Simon? (Mark 3:16)

A. Peter
B. John
C. James
D. Thaddeus

24. What name did Jesus give to James and John, the sons of Zebedee? (Mark 3:17)

A. Sons of Thunder
B. Sons of Fire
C. Sons of God
D. Sons of men

WEEK 2 MEMORY VERSE: MARK 9:23
Jesus said to him, "If you can believe, all things are possible to him who believes."

WEEK 2

25. What did the scribes mean when they accused Jesus of having Beelzebub? (Mark 3:22)

A. That He used satanic power to cast out demons
B. That He was possessed by the ruler of demons
C. Both A and B
D. That He was a magician

26. How did Jesus respond to the accusation that He had Beelzebub? (Mark 3:22–27

A. A kingdom divided against itself cannot stand
B. Satan cannot cast out Satan
C. You must first bind the strong man to plunder his house
D. All the above

27. Which of the following did Jesus say is unpardonable (unforgivable) sin? (Mark 3:28-29)

A. Blasphemy against God
B. Blasphemy against the Son of Man
C. Blasphemy against the Son of God
D. Blasphemy against the Holy Spirit

WEEK 2 MEMORY VERSE: MARK 9:23
Jesus said to him, "If you can believe, all things are possible to him who believes."

WEEK 2

28. What is the consequence of blaspheming the Holy Spirit? (Mark 3:29)

A. Sickness and pain
B. Endless spiritual battles
C. A cursed life
D. Eternal condemnation

29. Who did Jesus say are His true mother and brothers? (Mark 3:31–35)

A. His neighbors
B. His disciples
C. Mary and James
D. Whoever does the will of God

30. What happened to the seed that fell by the wayside? (Mark 4:3-4)

A. It was choked by thorns
B. Birds of the air came and devoured it
C. It produced fruit
D. It withered away because it had no root

WEEK 2 MEMORY VERSE: MARK 9:23
Jesus said to him, "If you can believe, all things are possible to him who believes."

WEEK 2

31. What happened to the seed that fell on stony places? (Mark 4:5-6)

A. It was choked by thorns
B. Birds of the air came and devoured it
C. It produced fruit
D. It withered away because it had no root

32. What happened to the seed that fell among thorns? (Mark 4:7)

A. It was choked by thorns
B. Birds of the air came and devoured it
C. It produced fruit
D. It withered away because it had no root

33. What happened to the seed that fell on good ground? (Mark 4:8)

A. It was choked by thorns
B. Birds of the air came and devoured it
C. It produced fruit
D. It withered away because it had no root

WEEK 2 MEMORY VERSE: MARK 9:23
Jesus said to him, "If you can believe, all things are possible to him who believes."

WEEK 2

34. Jesus said "To some, it has been given to understand the mysteries of the kingdom, but to others, all things come in parables" (Mark 4:10-12)

A. True
B. False

35. What does the seed by the wayside represent? (Mark 4:14–15)

A. Those who receive the Word but quickly fall away immediately problems arise
B. Those who accept the Word and bear much fruit
C. Those who hear the Word, but Satan immediately takes it away
D. Those who hear the word but it is choked by worldly distractions

36. What does the seed on stony ground represent? (Mark 4:16–17)

A. Those who receive the Word but quickly fall away immediately problems arise
B. Those who accept the Word and bear much fruit
C. Those who hear the Word, but Satan immediately takes it away
D. Those who hear the word but it is choked by worldly distractions

WEEK 2 MEMORY VERSE: MARK 9:23
Jesus said to him, "If you can believe, all things are possible to him who believes."

WEEK 2

37. What does the seed among thorns represent? (Mark 4:18–19)

A. Those who receive the Word but quickly fall away immediately problems arise
B. Those who accept the Word and bear much fruit
C. Those who hear the Word, but Satan immediately takes it away
D. Those who hear the word but it is choked by worldly distractions

38. What does the seed on good ground represent? (Mark 4:20)

A. Those who receive the Word but quickly fall away immediately problems arise
B. Those who accept the Word and bear much fruit
C. Those who hear the Word, but Satan immediately takes it away
D. Those who hear the word but it is choked by worldly distractions

39. What did Jesus teach about the mustard seed and the Kingdom of God? (Mark 4:30–32)

A. It starts small but grows into something large and life-giving
B. Only a few will enter heaven
C. The seed cannot be ignored
D. The mustard seed is magical

WEEK 2 MEMORY VERSE: MARK 9:23
Jesus said to him, "If you can believe, all things are possible to him who believes."

WEEK 2

40. What happened when Jesus met the man with many demons in the region of the Gadarenes? (Mark 5:1–17)

A. The demons begged Jesus not to torment them
B. Jesus sent them into a herd of pigs, which drowned
C. The people asked Jesus to leave their region
D. All the above

41. What is the meaning of the name "Legion" in the demon possessed man? (Mark 5:9)

A. They were many demons
B. They came from a place called Legion
C. They were known and feared everywhere
D. They were an ancient force of evil

42. When the healed man begged to go with Jesus, what did Jesus tell him? (Mark 5:18–19)

A. You are not yet ready to follow Me
B. Go home and tell your friends the great things the Lord has done for you
C. Sell all you have, then follow Me
D. Reconcile with your family and come back later

WEEK 2 MEMORY VERSE: MARK 9:23
Jesus said to him, "If you can believe, all things are possible to him who believes."

"

I will not fear, because
My God is with me
(Psalms 118:6)

"

Great job completing the week!

Did you memorize the daily verse?
Test yourself by writing it here...

_____

_____

_____

_____

_____

_____

Use this space to draw a scene from the Bible or reflect
on something you learned, felt or experienced...

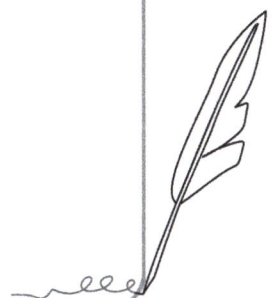

WEEK 3

43. Why did the woman with the issue of blood touch Jesus' garment? (Mark 5:25–28)

A. She was trying to get His attention
B. She believed that if she touched the Hem of His garment, she would be healed
C. She wanted Him to follow her home
D. It happened by accident in the crowd

44. What did Jesus say to the woman after she was healed of her bleeding? (Mark 5:34)

A. Why did you touch Me without asking?
B. You have great faith, like no other in Israel
C. I have healed you — go and be quiet about it
D. Daughter, your faith has made you well. Go in peace and be healed of your affliction

45. What was Jesus' response when He heard Jairus' daughter had died? (Mark 5:35–39)

A. Do not cry, she is with God
B. Do not be afraid; only believe
C. The child is not dead, but sleeping
D. Both B and C

WEEK 3 MEMORY VERSE: MARK 10:45
For even the Son of Man did not come to be served, but to serve, and to give His life a ransom for many.

WEEK 3

46. Why did the crowd laugh at Jesus when He came to Jairus' house? (Mark 5:39–40)

A. Because He said the girl was not dead, but sleeping
B. Because they didn't believe in miracles
C. Because they were mocking His authority
D. Because they thought He was confused

47. Which disciples did Jesus take with Him into Jairus' house? (Mark 5:37)

A. Peter, Andrew, and James
B. Peter, James, and John
C. Thomas, Simon, and Mark
D. James, John, and Matthew

48. What does "Talitha cumi" mean? (Mark 5:41)

A. Little girl, you are healed
B. Little girl, I say to you, arise
C. Young girl, your faith has made you well
D. Arise and live again

WEEK 3 MEMORY VERSE: MARK 10:45
For even the Son of Man did not come to be served, but to serve, and to give His life a ransom for many.

WEEK 3

49. How old was Jairus' daughter? (Mark 5:42)

A. 10 years old
B. 11 years old
C. 12 years old
D. 7 years old

50. Why were people offended when Jesus taught in His hometown? (Mark 6:1–3)

A. He spoke too boldly
B. He corrected them
C. He said things they didn't understand
D. They saw Him only as the carpenter's son and could not believe He was sent by God

51. Jesus said a prophet is honored everywhere except where? (Mark 6:4)

A. In foreign lands
B. In his hometown, among relatives, and in his own house
C. In front of kings
D. In the synagogue

WEEK 3 MEMORY VERSE: MARK 10:45
For even the Son of Man did not come to be served, but to serve, and to give His life a ransom for many.

WEEK 3

52. Why was Jesus unable to perform mighty miracles in Nazareth? (Mark 6:5–6)

A. They rejected His teaching
B. They asked Him to leave
C. Because of their unbelief
D. They didn't bring the sick to Him

53. What instructions did Jesus give the disciples when He sent them out two by two? (Mark 6:7–11)

A. Take nothing for the journey except a staff (walking stick)
B. Whatever home they entered, they were to stay there until they left the area
C. Whenever they were not welcomed, the disciples were to shake off the dust under their feet as a testimony against them
D. All the above

54. Who did King Herod believe Jesus was? (Mark 6:14)

A. Elijah
B. Isaiah
C. Micah
D. John the Baptist, risen from the dead

WEEK 3 MEMORY VERSE: MARK 10:45
For even the Son of Man did not come to be served, but to serve, and to give His life a ransom for many.

WEEK 3

55. Why did King Herod have John the Baptist arrested and put in prison? (Mark 6:17–18)

A. Because John boldly told Herod that it was sinful to marry Herodias, his brother Philip's wife
B. Because John refused to stop preaching in public
C. Because Herod feared John's growing influence
D. Because Herodias asked him to silence John

56. What kept Herod from putting John the Baptist to death sooner? (Mark 6:20)

A. He knew that John was a just and holy man
B. He knew John was Jesus' friend
C. Herod feared God
D. Herodias told him to wait

57. What caused King Herod to order the beheading of John the Baptist? (Mark 6:21–28)

A. Herod was influenced by John's enemies
B. Herodias' daughter danced before the king, and he made a rash vow to give her whatever she asked — and at her mother's urging, she asked for John's head
C. Herod was jealous of John's influence
D. Herod was tricked by his servants

WEEK 3 MEMORY VERSE: MARK 10:45
For even the Son of Man did not come to be served, but to serve, and to give His life a ransom for many.

WEEK 3

58. Why was Jesus moved with compassion when He saw the crowds? (Mark 6:34) (Mark 6:34)

A. They looked tired and hungry
B. They were like sheep without a shepherd
C. They had been waiting all day
D. They were seeking miracles

59. How much food did the disciples have when feeding the 5,000 men? (Mark 6:37–44)

A. 2 loaves and 5 fish
B. 2 fish and 5 loaves of bread
C. 12 baskets of fish
D. 7 loaves of bread and 2 fish

60. How much food remained after the 5000 men were fed? (Mark 6:42-44)

A. 12 baskets of fish
B. 7 baskets of bread
C. 10 baskets of crumbs
D. 12 baskets full of leftover fragments

WEEK 3 MEMORY VERSE: MARK 10:45
For even the Son of Man did not come to be served, but to serve, and to give His life a ransom for many.

WEEK 3

61. What happened when the sick were brought to Jesus in the land of Gennesaret? (Mark 6:53–56)

A. Jesus prayed for each one of them
B. Jesus commanded sickness to leave them
C. Jesus laid hands on them and they recovered
D. They begged to touch the hem of His garment, and all who touched Him were healed

62. How did Jesus respond when the Pharisees criticized His disciples for not washing hands before eating? (Mark 7:5–15)

A. He called them hypocrites for honoring traditions over God's commands
B. He said what defiles a person is not what goes in, but what comes out from the heart
C. He quoted Isaiah, saying they teach human ideas as if they were God's commands
D. All the above

63. How did Jesus explain why food does not defile a person? (Mark 7:17–23)

A. What enters the stomach is eliminated, but what comes from the heart defiles a person
B. Evil thoughts, sexual sins, pride, and deceit flow from the heart and defile a person
C. Both A and B
D. Jesus chose not to answer

WEEK 3 MEMORY VERSE: MARK 10:45
For even the Son of Man did not come to be served, but to serve, and to give His life a ransom for many.

"

Whatever I do, I do it heartily, as to the Lord and not to men (Colossians 3:23)

"

Great job completing the week!

**Did you memorize the daily verse?
Test yourself by writing it here...**

_____

_____

_____

_____

_____

_____

**Use this space to draw a scene from the Bible or reflect
on something you learned, felt or experienced...**

WEEK 4

64. What was the Syro-Phoenician woman's response when Jesus said the children's bread shouldn't be given to dogs? (Mark 7:25–28)

A. Yes, Lord, but even the little dogs eat the crumbs that fall from the children's table
B. She bowed in worship
C. She wept and pleaded for mercy
D. She ran to get more help

65. What did Jesus do to heal the boy who was deaf and had a speech impediment? (Mark 7:32–33)

A. He laid hands on him and prayed
B. He put His fingers in his ears, spat, and touched his tongue
C. He told him to touch His garment
D. He anointed him with oil

66. What did Jesus mean when He said "Ephphatha" to the deaf boy? (Mark 7:34)

A. Be healed
B. Be anointed
C. Be made whole
D. Be opened

WEEK 4 MEMORY VERSE: MARK 11:24
Therefore I say to you, whatever things you ask when you pray, believe that you receive them, and you will have them.

WEEK 4

67. How much food did the disciples have before Jesus fed the 4,000? (Mark 8:1–7)

A. 7 loaves and a few small fish
B. 5 loaves and 2 fish
C. 2 fish and 5 loaves
D. A few loaves and 7 fish

68. How much food was left over after the 4,000 were fed? (Mark 8:8)

A. 12 baskets of bread
B. 12 baskets of fish
C. 12 baskets of leftovers
D. 7 large baskets of leftovers

69. What did Jesus say when the Pharisees asked for a sign from heaven? (Mark 8:11–12)

A. He showed them a miracle
B. He said He was the sign
C. He told them to open their eyes
D. He said, "No sign shall be given to this generation"

WEEK 4 MEMORY VERSE: MARK 11:24
Therefore I say to you, whatever things you ask when you pray, believe that you receive them, and you will have them.

WEEK 4

70. How did Jesus heal the blind man at Bethsaida? (Mark 8:22-25)

A. He told him to go wash
B. He spat on his eyes and laid hands on him
C. He prayed from a distance
D. He sent him to the pool of Siloam

71. What did the blind man say after Jesus asked if he could see? (Mark 8:23–24)

A. I see shadows in the light
B. I see men like trees, walking
C. I see the wind and movement
D. I see light, but no faces

72. Who correctly answered Jesus' question, "Who do you say that I am?" and what did he say? (Mark 8:27–30)

A. Peter said, "You are the Christ"
B. James said, "You are the Son of the Living God"
C. Matthew said, "You are the Messiah"
D. John said, "You are the Savior of the world"

WEEK 4 MEMORY VERSE: MARK 11:24
Therefore I say to you, whatever things you ask when you pray, believe
that you receive them, and you will have them.

WEEK 4

73. Why did Jesus rebuke Peter? (Mark 8:31-33)

A. Peter doubted Jesus' power
B. Peter was being argumentative
C. Peter was focused on the things of man, not God's plan
D. Jesus was upset and lashed out

74. Which of these statements did Jesus NOT say? (Mark 8:34–38)

A. Whoever wants to save their life will lose it
B. What will it profit a man to gain the whole world and lose his soul?
C. Whoever is ashamed of Me, I will also be ashamed of him
D. I've got the whole world, the wind, and the rain in My hands

75. Which of the following disciples were not present when Jesus was transfigured? (Mark 9:2)

A. Peter
B. James
C. John
D. Luke

WEEK 4 MEMORY VERSE: MARK 11:24
Therefore I say to you, whatever things you ask when you pray, believe that you receive them, and you will have them.

WEEK 4

76. When Jesus was transfigured, His clothes became white like snow. What else happened? (Mark 9:2-8)

A. His clothes became shining white
B. Moses and Elijah appeared with Him
C. God's voice was heard saying ""This is my beloved Son, Hear Him!"
D. All the above

77. Why couldn't the disciples cast out the mute spirit from the boy? (Mark 9:17–29)

A. They forgot to pray
B. They were afraid
C. Jesus said this kind only comes out by prayer and fasting
D. They didn't believe

78. What was the father's response when Jesus said, "If you believe, all things are possible"? (Mark 9:23–24)

A. I have faith
B. I believe fully
C. Lord, I believe; help my unbelief
D. Help me to believe more

WEEK 4 MEMORY VERSE: MARK 11:24
Therefore I say to you, whatever things you ask when you pray, believe that you receive them, and you will have them.

WEEK 4

79. What did Jesus say when the disciples argued about who was the greatest? (Mark 9:33–35)

A. The least among you is the greatest
B. If anyone desires to be first, he must be last of all and servant of all
C. The greatest must deny themselves
D. Whoever follows Me the closest is the greatest

80. What did Jesus say about receiving little children? (Mark 9:37)

A. Whoever receives one of these little children in My name receives Me
B. Whoever receives Me, receives not Me but Him who sent Me
C. Both A and B
D. Whoever receives me, I will abide also in him

81. What did Jesus say when His disciples stopped a man from casting out demons in His name? (Mark 9:38–41)

A. Do not stop him, for no one who works a miracle in My name will soon speak evil of Me
B. He who is not against us is on our side
C. Whoever gives you a cup of water in My name will not lose their reward
D. All the above

WEEK 4 MEMORY VERSE: MARK 11:24
Therefore I say to you, whatever things you ask when you pray, believe that you receive them, and you will have them.

WEEK 4

82. What did Jesus say about causing a believing child to sin? (Mark 9:42)

A. It would be better if a large millstone were hung around his neck and he were thrown into the sea
B. He should repent before he's punished
C. He should be cut off from the people
D. He should ask for forgiveness

83. What did Jesus say to do if your hand, foot, or eye causes you to sin? (Mark 9:43–48)

A. Pray for strength
B. Cut it off or pluck it out—it is better to enter life maimed than be thrown into hell whole
C. Ask a prophet to intercede
D. Cry out for mercy

84. Which of the following are words Jesus spoke about salt and sacrifice? (Mark 9:49–50)

A. Everyone will be seasoned with fire
B. Salt is good, but if it loses its flavor, how can it be seasoned?
C. Have salt in yourselves and peace with one another
D. All the above

WEEK 4 MEMORY VERSE: MARK 11:24
Therefore I say to you, whatever things you ask when you pray, believe that you receive them, and you will have them.

"

The joy of the Lord is my strength (Nehemiah 8:10)

"

Great job completing the week!

Did you memorize the daily verse?
Test yourself by writing it here...

_____

_____

_____

_____

_____

Use this space to draw a scene from the Bible or reflect
on something you learned, felt or experienced...

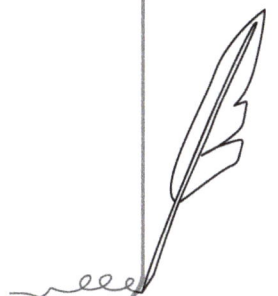

WEEK 5

85. What did Jesus say about divorce? (Mark 10:2–12)

A. What God joins together, let no man separate
B. Moses allowed divorce due to the hardness of hearts
C. Divorce followed by remarriage is adultery
D. All the above

86. How did Jesus compare little children to the Kingdom of God? (Mark 10:13–15)

A. Whoever does not receive the Kingdom like a child will not enter it
B. Only those who act like children can enter
C. Children automatically inherit the Kingdom
D. Children are innocent and favored

87. What did Jesus tell the rich young ruler to do after keeping the commandments? (Mark 10:17–21)

A. Sell everything he had
B. Give to the poor
C. Follow Jesus
D. Sell all he had, give to the poor, and follow Jesus to have treasure in heaven

WEEK 5 MEMORY VERSE: MARK 12:30
And you shall love the Lord your God with all your heart, with all your soul, with all your mind, and with all your strength.'
This is the first commandment.

WEEK 5

88. Jesus said it's hard for those who trust in riches to enter God's kingdom. What did He compare it to? (Mark 10:23–25)

A. Climbing a mountain
B. Passing through fire
C. A camel going through the eye of a needle
D. A door being closed forever

89. What was Jesus' response when the disciples asked, "Who then can be saved?" (Mark 10:26–27)

A. You must believe
B. With men it is impossible, but not with God; for with God all things are possible
C. You must be born again
D. All things are possible for the wise

90. What will those who have left all to follow Jesus receive? (Mark 10:28-31)

A. Earthly wealth and respect
B. A hundredfold return now, with persecutions—and eternal life in the age to come
C. Honor in heaven only
D. Glory and power on earth

WEEK 5 MEMORY VERSE: MARK 12:30
And you shall love the Lord your God with all your heart, with all your soul, with all your mind, and with all your strength.'
This is the first commandment.

WEEK 5

91. What did Jesus predict would happen to Him before His resurrection? (Mark 10:32–34)

A. He would be mocked
B. He would be scourged
C. He would be spit on
D. All the above

92. Who will sit at Jesus' right and left hand in heaven? (Mark 10:35–40)

A. Peter and John
B. Jesus said it would be James and John
C. It is not for Jesus to grant—it is for those for whom it is prepared
D. Jesus said Simon Peter would sit at His right

93. In the kingdom of heaven, what must one who desires to be great do? (Mark 10:43-44)

A. Those that desire to be great shall be servants
B. Those that desire to be first shall be slaves of all
C. Both A and B
D. We are all equal

WEEK 5 MEMORY VERSE: MARK 12:30
And you shall love the Lord your God with all your heart, with all your soul, with all your mind, and with all your strength.'
This is the first commandment.

WEEK 5

94. What did Jesus say was the purpose for which He came? (Mark 10:45)

A. To set the captives free
B. To show us the way
C. To pay our debts
D. To serve and to give His life a ransom for many

95. What did Jesus say to Bartimaeus after healing him? (Mark 10:46–52)

A. Go your way, your faith has made you well
B. Receive your sight
C. You are the healed of the Lord
D. Be restored

96. When Jesus and His disciples neared Jerusalem, what animal did He send for? (Mark 11:2)

A. A colt (young donkey)
B. A young ox
C. A lamb
D. A goat

WEEK 5 MEMORY VERSE: MARK 12:30
And you shall love the Lord your God with all your heart, with all your soul, with all your mind, and with all your strength.'
This is the first commandment.

WEEK 5

97. What did the disciples say when asked why they needed the animal? (Mark 11:3)

A. The Lord has need of it
B. It is part of prophecy
C. The Master rides it
D. We need it for worship

98. What happened as Jesus entered Jerusalem on the colt? (Mark 11:7–10)

A. The people shouted "Hosanna!"
B. They laid their clothes and branches on the road
C. They honored Him as the One sent by the Lord
D. All the above

99. What did Jesus teach after the fig tree withered? (Mark 11:20–24)

A. Have faith in God
B. Speak to mountains without doubting and they will obey
C. Believe when you pray and you will receive
D. All the above

WEEK 5 MEMORY VERSE: MARK 12:30
And you shall love the Lord your God with all your heart, with all your soul, with all your mind, and with all your strength.'
This is the first commandment.

WEEK 5

100. Why does Jesus urge us to forgive others? (Mark 11:25-26)

A) That our Father in Heaven may also forgive us our sins
B) If we do not forgive, neither will our Father in Heaven forgive our sins
C) Both A and B
D) So we can feel better

101. Which Scripture did Jesus quote to explain the parable of the wicked vinedressers? (Mark 12:1–11)

A. "The stone which the builders rejected has become the chief cornerstone"
B. "I was hungry, and you did not feed Me"
C. "Give, and it will be given to you"
D. "I am the vine; you are the branches"

102. What did Jesus say about marriage in the resurrection when asked about the woman who had seven husbands? (Mark 12:18–25)

A. She will return to the first husband
B. All the husbands will be joined to her
C. None will be joined to her, she will remain single
D. In the resurrection, they neither marry nor are given in marriage, but are like angels in heaven

WEEK 5 MEMORY VERSE: MARK 12:30
And you shall love the Lord your God with all your heart, with all your soul, with all your mind, and with all your strength.'
This is the first commandment.

WEEK 5

103. What did Jesus teach about the resurrection using God's statement to Moses? (Mark 12:26–27)

A. God is the God of the living and not the dead
B. God is concerned about Abraham, Isaac, and Jacob
C. God blesses every righteous generation
D. Resurrection only applies to saints

104. What is the first and greatest commandment? (Mark 12:28–30)

A. Love the Lord your God with all your heart, soul, mind, and strength
B. Love your neighbor as yourself
C. Keep the Sabbath holy
D. Both A and B

105. What question did Jesus ask to teach the Scribes about Christ being David's Lord? (Mark 12:35–37)

A. How then does David by the Holy Spirit call Him Lord, saying, "The Lord said to my Lord, sit at my right hand till I make your enemies your footstool."
B. If David calls Him Lord, how is He his Son?
C. Both A and B
D. Is Joseph the carpenter, my father?

WEEK 5 MEMORY VERSE: MARK 12:30
And you shall love the Lord your God with all your heart, with all your soul, with all your mind, and with all your strength.'
This is the first commandment.

"

With me are riches and honor, enduring wealth and prosperity (Proverbs 8:18)

"

Great job completing the week!

Did you memorize the daily verse?
Test yourself by writing it here...

_____

_____

_____

_____

_____

_____

Use this space to draw a scene from the Bible or reflect on something you learned, felt or experienced...

WEEK 6

106. What did Jesus say about the Scribes who will receive greater condemnation? (Mark 12:38–40)

A. They love to wear long robes and love greetings in the marketplaces
B. They seek places of honor
C. They devour widows' houses and make long prayers to look holy
D. All the above

107. Why did Jesus praise the widow who gave two mites? (Mark 12:41–44)

A. While others gave out of their abundance, she gave out of her poverty
B. She gave all that she had
C. She gave her whole livelihood (everything she had to live on)
D. All the above

108. Which of the following is NOT mentioned as a sign of the end times? (Mark 13:5–8)

A. There will be all kinds of sicknesses and diseases
B. Many will deceive others by claiming to be the Messiah
C. There will be wars and rumors of war
D. Nations will rise against nations and kingdoms against kingdoms

WEEK 6 MEMORY VERSE: MARK 13:31
Heaven and earth will pass away, but My words will by no means pass away.

WEEK 6

109. What did Jesus tell the disciples to do when arrested for His name's sake? (Mark 13:11)

A. They shoud speak what is given to them by the Holy Spirit at that hour
B. They should say nothing
C. They should be very brief
D. They should be strong and courageous

110. Which prophet spoke about the abomination of desolation? (Mark 13:14)

A. Isaiah
B. Jeremiah
C. Daniel
D. Micah

111. How did Jesus describe the great tribulation? (Mark 13:14-19

A. Let him who is on the housetop not go down into the house, nor enter to take anything out of his house
B. Let him who is in the field not go back to get his clothes
C. Woe to pregnant and nursing babies
D. All the above

WEEK 6 MEMORY VERSE: MARK 13:31
Heaven and earth will pass away, but My words will by no means pass away.

WEEK 6

112. Will the days of tribulation be shortened? Why? (Mark 13:20)

A. Yes, for the sake of the elect
B. Yes, for a final call to repentance
C. No, judgment will be complete
D. No, God does not change His plans

113. What will happen to the sun, moon, stars, and heavens after the tribulation? (Mark 13:24-25)

A. All will shine brightly
B. The heavens will rejoice
C. The sun will be darkened, the moon won't give light, the stars will fall, and powers in the heavens will be shaken
D. They will tremble and fade

114. What did Jesus say about His second coming? (Mark 13:26–27)

A. He will appear suddenly
B. There will be trumpets and clouds
C. He will come in the clouds with power and glory, and the angels will gather His elect
D. He will rule from Jerusalem

WEEK 6 MEMORY VERSE: MARK 13:31
Heaven and earth will pass away, but My words will by no means pass away.

WEEK 6

115. How did Jesus compare the fig tree to His return?
(Mark 13:28–29)

A. The fig tree represents Israel
B. Just as you know summer is near when the fig tree puts forth leaves, so will the signs point to His coming
C. The fig tree bears fruit suddenly
D. His return is in the springtime

116. Jesus said that heaven and earth will pass away, but
_____ will by no means pass away (Mark 13:30-31)

A. His miracles
B. His love
C. His words
D. His covenant with Israel

117. Who knows the day and hour of the return of the Son of Man?
(Mark 13:32)

A. Only God the Father
B. God the Father and the Holy Spirit
C. Jesus and the angels
D. The chosen prophets

WEEK 6 MEMORY VERSE: MARK 13:31
Heaven and earth will pass away, but My words will by no means pass away.

WEEK 6

118. What did Jesus advise us to do about His coming? (Mark 13:33)

A. Fast and pray
B. Watch and stay alert
C. Ask God for discernment
D. Ask God for revelation

119. After what feast did Jesus say He would be betrayed and crucified? (Mark 14:1)

A. The Feast of the Tabernacles
B. The Pentecost
C. The Passover and Feast of Unleavened Bread
D. The Feast of Dedication

120. Why did Jesus speak well of the woman who poured oil on Him from an alabaster flask? (Mark 14:3–8)

A. She honored Him instead of selling the oil
B. She prepared His body for burial
C. She gave sacrificially
D. All the above

WEEK 6 MEMORY VERSE: MARK 13:31
Heaven and earth will pass away, but My words will by no means pass away.

WEEK 6

121. Which of Jesus' disciples agreed to betray Him? (Mark 14:10)

A. James
B. Peter
C. Judas Iscariot
D. John

122. How did Jesus identify the one who would betray Him? (Mark 14:17–20)

A. The one who sat closest to Him
B. The one who dipped his hand in the dish with Him
C. The one who kissed His cheek
D. The one who whispered in His ear

123. What scripture was fulfilled when Jesus said His disciples would stumble because of Him? (Mark 14:27–28)

A. "I will strike the Shepherd, and the sheep will be scattered"
B. "Your word is a lamp to my feet"
C. "Those who love Your law have great peace"
D. "You will walk in safety and not stumble"

WEEK 6 MEMORY VERSE: MARK 13:31
Heaven and earth will pass away, but My words will by no means pass away.

WEEK 6

124. Jesus predicted that one of His disciples would deny knowing him _____ times before the rooster crows (Mark 14:29-30)

A. Peter, 3 times
B. John, 3 Times
C. Peter, 7 times
D. John, 7 times

125. What is the name of the place where Jesus went to pray before His arrest? (Mark 14:32)

A. Mount of Olives
B. Gethsemane
C. Eden
D. Golgotha

126. Which disciples did Jesus take with Him to pray in Gethsemane? (Mark 14:33)

A. Peter
B. James
C. John
D. All the above

WEEK 6 MEMORY VERSE: MARK 13:31
Heaven and earth will pass away, but My words will by no means pass away.

"

I am willing and obedient, therefore I shall eat the good of the land (Isaiah 1:19)

"

Great job completing the week!

Did you memorize the daily verse?
Test yourself by writing it here...

_____

_____

_____

_____

_____

_____

Use this space to draw a scene from the Bible or reflect on something you learned, felt or experienced...

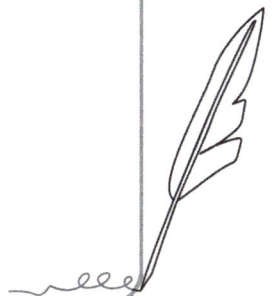

WEEK 7

127. What did Jesus pray in the garden before His arrest?
(Mark 14:36)

A. Abba, Father, take this cup from Me
B. Not what I will, but what You will
C. Our Father in Heaven, hallowed be Your name
D. Both A and B

128. Why did Jesus tell the disciples to watch and pray?
(Mark 14:38)

A. So that they would not give in to temptation because the spirit is willing but the flesh is weak
B. So that Jesus would not have to suffer
C. So that Jesus would not be crucified
D. All the above

129. What sign did Judas give the chief priests to identify Jesus?
(Mark 14:43–44)

A. A handshake
B. A kiss
C. A whispered greeting
D. A bow

WEEK 7 MEMORY VERSE: MARK 16:15
And He said to them, "Go into all the world and preach the gospel to every creature.

WEEK 7

130. What did Jesus say when false accusations were made against Him at the high priest's council? (Mark 14:55–61)

A. He defended Himself
B. He called them hypocrites
C. He denied all charges
D. He remained silent

131. What sin was Jesus falsely accused of that led to His death? (Mark 14:61–64)

A. Blasphemy
B. Deceiving the people
C. Stirring up rebellion
D. Healing on the Sabbath

132. Why did Peter weep after the rooster crowed? (Mark 14:66–72)

A. He saw Jesus suffering
B. He couldn't find the other disciples
C. He had denied Jesus three times, just as Jesus said
D. He felt helpless

WEEK 7 MEMORY VERSE: MARK 16:15
And He said to them, "Go into all the world and preach the gospel to every creature.

WEEK 7

133. What was Jesus' response when accused before Pilate? (Mark 15:3–5)

A. He asked for mercy
B. He declared the truth
C. He defended Himself
D. He remained silent

134. Who was released instead of Jesus, and what was his crime? (Mark 15:6–15)

A. Barabbas, a murderer
B. Barabbas, a thief
C. Beelzebub, a thief, and murderer
D. Bartholomew, a murderer

135. Which of the following is NOT something the soldiers did to mock Jesus? (Mark 15:17–20)

A. Put a purple robe on Him
B. Twisted a crown of thorns
C. Struck Him with a reed and mocked Him
D. Removed His sandals

WEEK 7 MEMORY VERSE: MARK 16:15
And He said to them, "Go into all the world and preach the gospel to every creature.

WEEK 7

136. Who was forced to help Jesus carry His cross? (Mark 15:21)

A. Peter
B. John
C. Simon of Cyrene
D. Matthew

137. What is the name of the place where Jesus was crucified? (Mark 15:22)

A. Gethsemane
B. Golgotha
C. Goliath
D. Jerusalem

138. What does "Golgotha" mean? (Mark 15:22)

A. Place of judgment
B. Place of a skull
C. Place of sorrow
D. Place of gnashing

WEEK 7 MEMORY VERSE: MARK 16:15
And He said to them, "Go into all the world and preach the gospel to every creature.

WEEK 7

139. What did the soldiers give Jesus to drink at Golgotha? (Mark 15:23)

A. Water
B. Wine mixed with myrrh
C. Bitter vinegar
D. Grape juice

140. What was the accusation written against Jesus and placed on His cross? (Mark 15:26)

A. This is Jesus
B. This is Jesus the blasphemer
C. The King of the Jews
D. This is the Son of God

141. Who was crucified alongside Jesus? (Mark 15:27)

A. Two robbers, one on His right and one on His left
B. Two murderers
C. A single thief
D. A Roman soldier

WEEK 7 MEMORY VERSE: MARK 16:15
And He said to them, "Go into all the world and preach the gospel to every creature.

WEEK 7

142. What Scripture was fulfilled when Jesus was crucified with sinners? (Mark 15:28)

A. He was numbered with the transgressors
B. The wages of sin is death
C. All have sinned and fallen short of the glory of God
D. A righteous man dies for the wicked

143. How did the people mock Jesus while He hung on the cross? (Mark 15:29–32)

A. They challenged Him to save Himself
B. They told Him to come down if He was King
C. They mocked His claim to destroy and rebuild the temple
D. All the above

144. What happened from the sixth hour to the ninth hour after Jesus was crucified? (Mark 15:33)

A. There was mourning
B. Angels wept
C. Darkness covered the whole land
D. A great earthquake shook the earth

WEEK 7 MEMORY VERSE: MARK 16:15
And He said to them, "Go into all the world and preach the gospel to every creature.

WEEK 7

145. At the ninth hour, what did Jesus cry out? (Mark 15:34)

A. "Eli, Eli, lama sabachthani?"
B. "My God, My God, why have You forsaken Me?"
C. Both A and B
D. "God forgive them"

146. When Jesus cried out, who did some people think He was calling? (Mark 15:35–36)

A. Elijah
B. Moses
C. Isaiah
D. David

147. What happened immediately after Jesus gave up His spirit? (Mark 15:37–38)

A. The people ran away
B. The veil of the temple was torn in two from top to bottom
C. The ground shook
D. The guards arrested the disciples

WEEK 7 MEMORY VERSE: MARK 16:15
And He said to them, "Go into all the world and preach the gospel to every creature.

148. Which women were present, watching Jesus' crucifixion from a distance? (Mark 15:40)

A. Mary Magdalene
B. Mary, the mother of James and Joseph
C. Salome, the mother of the sons of Zebedee
D. All the above

149. What was the name of the prominent man who for the body of Jesus so that he would bury Him? (Mark 15:43)

A. Joseph of Galilee
B. Joseph the Nazarene
C. Joseph of Cupertino
D. Joseph of Arimathea

150. What did Joseph do with Jesus' body? (Mark 15:46)

A. He wrapped it in fine linen
B. He laid it in a tomb cut from rock
C. He rolled a stone over the entrance
D. All the above

WEEK 7 MEMORY VERSE: MARK 16:15

And He said to them, "Go into all the world and preach the gospel to every creature.

BONUS QUESTIONS

151. Which women were first to go to the tomb and learn of Jesus' resurrection? (Mark 16:1)

A. Mary Magdalene
B. Mary, mother of James
C. Salome
D. All the above

152. Who announced that Jesus had risen? (Mark 16:5-6)

A. Jesus Himself
B. A booming voice from heaven
C. A young man clothed in white — an angel of the Lord
D. The centurion at the cross

153. To whom did Jesus first appear after His resurrection? (Mark 16:9)

A. Mary Magdalene, from whom He had cast out seven demons
B. Simon
C. Peter
D. John

WEEK 7 MEMORY VERSE: MARK 16:15
And He said to them, "Go into all the world and preach the gospel to every creature.

BONUS QUESTIONS

154. What did Jesus command the disciples after His resurrection? (Mark 16:15–16)

A. Go into all the world and preach the gospel to every creature.
B. Those who believe and are baptized will be saved
C. Both A and B
D. Forgive all those that persecuted me

155. What signs did Jesus say would follow those who believe? (Mark 16:17–18)

A. They will cast out demons and speak in new tongues
B. They will take up serpents and drink poison without being harmed
C. They will lay hands on the sick and they will recover
D. All the above

156. What happened after Jesus resurrected and had finished speaking to His disciples? (Mark 16:19-20)

A. He disappeared
B. He went into hiding
C. He was received up into heaven and sat at the right hand of God
D. The disciples scattered again

WEEK 7 MEMORY VERSE: MARK 16:15
And He said to them, "Go into all the world and preach the gospel to every creature.

"

Christ redeemed me from the curse of the law by becoming a curse for me (Galatians 3:13)

"

Great job completing the week!

**Did you memorize the daily verse?
Test yourself by writing it here...**

_____

_____

_____

_____

_____

**Use this space to draw a scene from the Bible or reflect
on something you learned, felt or experienced...**

Certificate of Completion

This Certificate Certifies That:

_____

Has Successfully Completed The Mark Workbook!

Flo & Grace

_____   _____

PARENT/TEACHER SIGNATURE   **PROJECT KINGDOM COME**

WOULD YOU LIKE TO ACCEPT JESUS INTO YOUR HEART?

THE BIBLE SAYS:

If you confess with your mouth that Jesus is Lord and believe in your heart that God has raised Him from the dead, you will be saved
(Romans 10:9)

SAY THE PRAYER BELOW OUT LOUD AND BELIEVE IT IN YOUR HEART!

Dear Lord Jesus,
I know that I am a sinner, and I ask for Your forgiveness.
I believe You died for my sins and rose from the dead.
I repent of my sins and invite You to come into my heart and life.
I want to trust and follow You as my Lord and Savior. Help me to live for you for the rest of my life.
I am now a child of God, and I ask You to fill me with Your Holy Spirit.

In Jesus' Name I pray, Amen.

Congratulations!
If you have prayed this prayer, please let an adult know or send an email to mybibleworkbooks@gmail.com

ANSWER KEY:

1. D	13. D	25. C
2. B	14. A	26. D
3. A	15. C	27. D
4. B	16. D	28. D
5. D	17. C	29. D
6. B	18. C	30. B
7. A	19. D	31. D
8. D	20. C	32. A
9. A	21. D	33. C
10. C	22. D	34. A
11. C	23. A	35. C
12. A	24. A	36. A

37. D	49. C	61. D
38. B	50. D	62. D
39. A	51. B	63. C
40. D	52. C	64. A
41. A	53. D	65. B
42. B	54. D	66. D
43. B	55. A	67. A
44. D	56. A	68. D
45. D	57. B	69. D
46. A	58. B	70. B
47. B	59. B	71. B
48. B	60. D	72. A

73. C	85. D	97. A
74. D	86. A	98. D
75. D	87. D	99. D
76. D	88. C	100. C
77. C	89. B	101. A
78. C	90. B	102. D
79. B	91. D	103. A
80. C	92. C	104. A
81. D	93. C	105. C
82. A	94. D	106. D
83. B	95. A	107. D
84. D	96. A	108. A

ANSWER KEY:

109. A	121. C	133. D
110. C	122. B	134. A
111. D	123. A	135. D
112. A	124. A	136. C
113. C	125. B	137. B
114. C	126. D	138. B
115. B	127. D	139. B
116. C	128. A	140. C
117. A	129. B	141. A
118. B	130. D	142. A
119. C	131. A	143. D
120. D	132. C	144. C

145. C

146. A

147. B

148. D

149. D

150. D

151. D

152. C

153. A

154. C

155. D

156. C

PLEASE GIVE US YOUR FEEDBACK!

Please send us your feedback on this workbook. We would love to hear what you enjoyed most, and ways you think it could be improved!

Please Send an email to: MyBibleWorkbooks@gmail.com, or leave us a comment on one of our social media pages.

MyBibleWorkbooks@gmail.com

Projectkingdomcome

Projectkingdomcome

SCAN ME

"

And I am certain that God, who began the good work within you, will continue His work until it is finally finished on the day when Christ Jesus returns.
Philippians 1:6

"

DRAW HERE

DRAW HERE

DRAW HERE

DRAW HERE

www.ingramcontent.com/pod-product-compliance
Lightning Source LLC
Chambersburg PA
CBHW061410090426
42740CB00026B/3492